# Inner Cities of Gulls
## J.P. DANCING BEAR

**salmon**poetry

Published in 2010 by
Salmon Poetry
Cliffs of Moher, County Clare, Ireland
Website: www.salmonpoetry.com
Email: info@salmonpoetry.com

Copyright © J.P. Dancing Bear, 2010

ISBN 978-1-907056-23-9

All rights reserved. No part of this publication may be reproduced or transmitted in any form or by any means, electronic or mechanical, including photography, recording, or any information storage or retrieval system, without permission in writing from the publisher. The book is sold subject to the condition that it shall not, by way of trade or otherwise, be lent, resold or otherwise circulated without the publisher's prior consent in any form of binding or cover other than that in which it is published and without a similar condition, including this condition, being imposed on the subsequent purchaser.

Cover artwork: *"Heaven" by Franziska Turek*
*http://franziskaturek.exto.nl/*
Cover design & typesetting: *Siobhán Hutson*
Printed in England by imprint*digital*.net

always for rain

# Acknowledgements

The author would like to give his thanks to the editors of the following magazines for publishing poems from this collection:

*Alehouse, Baltimore Review, Cave Wall, Cider Press Review, Concrete Wolf, Conspire, Cranky, Eclectica, Ellipsis, The Evansville Review, Full Circle Journal, Hotel Amerika, Into The Teeth of the Wind, In The Grove, The MacGuffin, Marlboro Review, Mississippi Review, The National Poetry Review, Pacific Review, Passager, Pebble Lake Review, Pilgrimage, Poems & Plays, Prairie Star, Quatro, Rattle, Redactions, Slipstream, Tifferet, Valparaiso Poetry Review, WOW*, and *Zuzu's Petals.*

"Making Fire" also appeared in *Red, White and Blues: poets on the promise of America* (Univesity of Iowa Press, 2004).

"Iago, the Poet", "Caliban" and "A Heart-Shaped Island" appeared in *In A Fine Frenzy: poets respond to Shakespeare* (University of Iowa Press, 2005)

"Fog Through a Bridge" appeared in *Blue Arc West: An Anthology of California Poets* (Tebot Bach, 2007)

"A Brief Informal History" also appeared in *After Shocks: The Poetry of Recovery for Life-Shattering Events* (Sante Lucia Books, 2008)

"The Winter Wolf" appeared in *Agreeable Friends: An Animal Anthology* (Moon Pie Press, 2008)

"What Language", "Caliban", "Making Fire", "Dia de Los Muertos", "Working" and "Citizen Kane" were all included in the chapbook, *What Language* (Slipstream, 2002).

"A Brief Informal History" and "Fog Through a Bridge" also appear in *Fieralingue* [Italy].

"Iago, the Poet", "Sky of Sleep", "Island Myths", "On Falling and Failing" and "West Nile" also appeared in *Verse Daily.*

# Contents

## I. Dust and a Scorpion

| | |
|---|---|
| Dia de los Muertos | 11 |
| Belief About a Barn and Silo | 12 |
| A Brief Informal History | 13 |
| Prospero, King of the City | 14 |
| From the Stolen Book of Firsts | 15 |
| Trepanning the Dust | 16 |
| Sisyphus Has Time For One More Question | 17 |
| Heart-Shaped Island | 18 |
| Silent Night | 19 |
| Iago, the Poet | 20 |
| Notes to Strangers | 21 |
| Naked | 23 |
| Turning Bird | 24 |
| Perseus in the Garden | 25 |
| Afraidness | 26 |
| A Bird History | 27 |
| Why Autumn is the Color of Stone | 28 |
| The Mud Weavers | 29 |

## II. Roots of Ash

| | |
|---|---|
| Caliban | 33 |
| West Nile | 34 |
| Citizen Kane | 35 |
| What if Hamlet had Drowned Instead of Ophelia | 36 |
| The Magician's Assistant | 37 |
| On Falling and Failing | 38 |
| Iago Says | 39 |
| The Dark Current | 40 |
| Sinking | 41 |
| Fog Through a Bridge | 42 |

| | |
|---|---|
| Prospero as TV Weatherman | 43 |
| Present Tension | 44 |
| After the Puma | 45 |
| Why Orpheus Could Not Stay Underground | 46 |
| Lake Light | 47 |
| Uncertainty Principle | 48 |
| What is Kept in the Heart of the Stone | 49 |

## III. In Defense of Love

| | |
|---|---|
| In Defense of Love | 53 |
| Making Fire | 63 |
| Private Symbology | 64 |
| Sky of Sleep | 66 |
| Night as a Love Poem | 67 |
| The Winter Wolf | 68 |
| Coyote Night | 69 |
| The Marriage of Tempest and Terra | 70 |
| What Language | 71 |
| Working | 72 |
| Coyote and Finch Aubade | 73 |
| Island Myths | 74 |
| When We Turned the House Into a Ship | 75 |
| Honey and Gratitude | 77 |
| *Author Biography* | *81* |

# I. Dust and a Scorpion

## Dia de los Muertos

When we finally lie down
let peace cover our bodies,
let a fine dust and a scorpion
wander in our pelvic bones.

Our skulls will bend to touch
at the forehead, as we did
each night. Our ribs will clasp
like praying fingers,
no black bead strand, no cross.

As our arms rest
on each others' shoulders
we will dance.
That night, my Love, we'll move
across the ballroom glitter
of the indigo sky.

# Belief About a Barn and Silo

As if the river of sun-colored grass
laps against the barn and its silo

to listen to the field mice sing a hymn
to the darkness of a wooden sky—

*Oh gracious God, our thanks for the gift
of hawkless air.* But maybe the field

has come to reclaim its small brown bodies
taking them back to the belly of soil.

The mice are not without their skeptics,
those who question God

for providing a roof but bringing the devil
in the green eyes of feral cats.

The debate rages through generations
amongst the quiet farm equipment

which in another time would have kept
the field calmed into canals of tilled soil,

would have forced the mice to a moonlit
exodus into the woods of waiting owls.

All of this memory and lore forces the
congregation to believe everything

has a purpose: the field floods forward
with a reason; the tractor sleeps by God's

design; the silo's silent air must be
sacred; and a cat's belly is surely hell.

# A Brief Informal History

For us, there was never a Harry Houdini
who escaped from the boxes or from behind
the Bureau of Land Management fences.
There was Jim Thorpe, who ran in circles

better than anyone else. He ran like a caged wolf.
That was something we all knew.

Great fists rose from the west, drifted over
the plains and pounded us with thunder
as though we had always been corn

waiting to be reduced to meal in the unfurling fields.
Out of the east the real fists came.

From within the snowstorm of lies, we heard
tales of our own resistance. But we heard

too, the names of our fathers embossed in chrome
on the fenders of cars, on the labels of alcohol,
in the lonely glow of neon above cafes. We heard
the death song coming from the sky, loud
and piercing the way a bird of iron might sound.

And all our ghosts. Those boys who went to war
and fought like there might be a freedom hidden
somewhere in blood. They came back to our open-
armed ghostfathers, their faces yellowed
and parched by the long poverty of their lives.

Our boys went back to being unneeded as a stone—
waiting in the desert, petroglyph for all that is lost.

# Prospero, King of the City

The city vibrates. The city purrs. Prospero has taken
to divining the future with Scrabble tiles.
He reclines on the bed in his penthouse; the afternoon
sun picking up speed before its inevitable crash.
The smell from the wharf wafts through the window.
On the street below, a drunk in a tailored suit argues
with a doorman about a dream of great ruined cities in the West.
People sound to Prospero like cartoon characters.

Someone honks a car horn, as if to signify the start
of a great migration north. There is a screech of brakes,
the pounding on the hood, yelling and more honking.
San Francisco is beginning to crumble into the sea.
It is because Prospero has messed the tiles up again.
At the curb comes a rumor about a rain of toads.
People on the street are strutting with a hip-hop gait
now—suggesting something great but final.

It's Christmas Eve; there's not another Scrabble set left
in the stores. The city's veins are trancing with traffic.
Lights smudge as fog creeps in through the Sunset district.
The cartoon men have everything Prospero ever wanted
or thought he deserved. They're laughing, belting out carols
as they huddle around a garbagecan fire, sharing a bottle.
A fat three-fingered hand throws in one wooden tile at a time—
someone calls out X and another ten points goes on the pyre.

# From the Stolen Book of Firsts

I slipped into the field where stood the first horse
to be freshly harnessed — angered by the ape
master. O opposable thumb, enslaving the species
around it, enslaving other thumbs. Someone
dipped a brush from horse hair and painted the history
of domination on a cave wall. A spear piercing the heart
of the great boar, the mastodon, wildebeests, gazelles—
another hand painted the daily specials on the menu
in a sanguine alphabet of hunger-lust. Drawn the ox
drawing a plow through the fields of the Nile valley
with its backdrop of slaves pulling another stone
into place on a pyramid. Then the need for a word
that described the taste of saltiness created an alphabet.
Twenty ingots of salt traded for two bales of cotton,
three ampoules of dyes made from powdered plants,
five vessels of wine, and two cows. The first word
on the papyrus said Bend, and next to it was a list
of animals, plants, landscapes, rivers and people.

# Trepanning the Dust

There is always dust and the surrender to it—
giving up and no longer cleaning after the dry rain
and falling leaves—let the wind do its part,

and let the forgetting begin, and the forgotten
step closer to ruin.  Here a people shrugged
and threw their hands in the air, then slouched

away, to some place different: the land of fresh
starts—vacated, no doubt, by another people
who could no longer live the way they always had.

So a coat of dust settles on the tools left behind,
stored in their earthy beds, waiting for the brush
of an archeologist, his breath dampening

the surface with his fascination over the hilts,
*You see: they used this edge to slice the skull
(Trepanning); and this long one to prod the brain back
to thinking like the rest of them had.*

# Sisyphus Has Time For One More Question

Listen, the rock was enough, I had dreams
that maybe I was wearing it down, the stone-
dust on my hands made hope hundreds
of years might grind it to a pebble—
a bit of grit in a bird's gut to help digest
the diet of seed and worm.  So I lift, push,
shoulder the boulder higher up the grade
almost happy for its shade in summer sun.
Wisp and hush of my palms on the rough
surface sounds like so many unhappy dead.
It was never the rock that emptied my chest
but the gods pushing back on the other side.

# Heart-Shaped Island

Prospero kept the island as his heart—
a secluded place far from the sight of ships
yet tensed, the open maw of a steel trap.
Scattered along the craggy shorelines
the planks of wrecked vessels drifted,
gray gulls cried like grieving sailors.
The underbrush rustled with dumb lust
as brutes smashed and searched in hunger.
At dusk gnats rose out of the reeds,
dark ghosts readying their haunts.
He left the night to the creatures
with their savage cacophony, each sure
it ruled the island, sure as his revenge.

# Silent Night

Jesus trembles in his step; he is passing
every Christ on the street; in fading daylight,
tiny messiahs sprout from between his ribs.

Shortly Jesus will take the cup of his hand
and protect the sleeping kings of the alleyways
and talk to the sick—silhouetted by the fallen

sun, all the sons of God will rise to form the horn
of an angel. They will gather and sing in the old tongue
before casting off, scattering, carried by tides—

the frail craft of their bodies on the rough waters
—who would believe this—all their walking
everywhere and the gulls soaring halos overhead.

Jesus keeps to his march past the doves, the lambs,
the burning thorns of his shadow, the department
store Jesus dressing windows, the whistling Jesus

in uniform, nurse Jesus with her white shoes, the
stickball Jesuses playing in their cul-de-sac, Jesus
of the taxicab who asks, *where to*, and the wet cement

walking Jesus stares at the winter night sky, the peaceful
first flake spiraling down. He is the birth of snow,
the silent relief, heavy blanket, the promise of heaven
to the sick, suffering, sleeping Jesuses of the street.

# Iago, the Poet

First, let me say it is sickening, this syrupy public
adoration for being homespun and common
tongued, master of the art.  I tire of his shotgunning metaphors
to stuff and mount on his study wall.
Last night I convinced a group of drunken bards to burn a pile
of his essays and his effigy while slamming down more beer
and shouting, you're not our leader!  Today I made the surrealists
believe he would come after them next and they should join
the language poets and attack first.  I've tricked his confidants
into thinking he's used them.  I have convinced his fans
he's insincere, a stage clambering phony who borrows
ideas, has roots in the greeting card business.  But my best
yet was swaying him to see his great love as a cheap
whore for hacks, charlatans and poseurs; and ruin his own career.

## Notes to Strangers

She leaves a man in the inner city of Gulls.
On the train she writes letters to strangers.
At each mail stop, another is posted:
>Dear Someone,
>I will not be home for sunset.
>I have eaten the last fruit from our tree,
>but am still too hungry to think of the past.
>All the boxes you sent were lost—sorry.
>I dreamed you were someone different
>last night, and I woke up in a panic.
>Always thinking of you,
>>—Love,
>>Guess Who

She kisses each stamp, closes each envelope
before settling into the rhythm of motion over rails.
The landscape went ribboning past—one never knows
what to write on a train, the sensations—
Of the sounds and vibrations? The sights?
Sentimentalities? —Or should she focus
on her thoughts? Or swim the moonlit pool
of her feelings? Love never wore her bathing suit.
Still, much to be said between the last stop and the next.

Today she felt like her notes needed a green pen,
something with the flare of a spring day,
as autumn crunched outside.
The tendrils of her Y's and G's dangles down
the trellis blue lines of her notebook.
Not every letter was the same, some subtler
differences than others.
*I have canned all the fruit of our tree,*
she smiles remembering the first
steaming aroma of cooking apple butter.
*All the boxes we packed were stolen—I wept for days.*

Such regret and yet the clouds could buffalo across the blues.
Form letters these were not.   What would be the point?
Each name from the phone book had music:
. . . *Steven Metheney . . . Matthew Donahue . . .*
     *Claudia De Paul . . .*
The envelope was addressed and stared blankly at her
as she wrote out, *I've always believed in you,*
dreaming that somewhere a person can get a note,
something knocking on the glass silence of their lives,
—an acknowledgment— even if it was only a porter
checking your boarding pass.

# Naked

I hear the cawing crow of desire rise
from its ashes again. She stands,
a master painter's model, peering down,
hair flash-flooding on one shoulder.
The apples behind her hang bewitchingly
and I want to say some thing perfect,
recite the litany of all things
that can be compared to each branch
of her body. Her skin is smooth
sculpted marble. Words fall away,
entire libraries burn: great frescos,
treaties and declarations, the natural
history of a continent lost to a spark.
And I stand here the happy owner
of a charred matchstick, still
fixed on her form, unconcerned,
consumed, ready to return to ashes
and wait for her nakedness again.

# Turning Bird

By the muddy banks of Winter
pushing to the ocean, I saw it there
through the bare fingered trees
against another storm. It flapped
against the sky, a small figure
tied and struggling
with an enormous weight. The myths
were never clear about it,
they only said that there was a bird
who turned the world.

I had always imagined such a job
assigned to the powerful wings
of an eagle or a hawk,
but never to a sparrow.
I stood where the tether emerged
from the ground
and heard no sound of straining
from the earth or its bird.

I watched for a long time
and felt what it must be like
to discover the theorized catalyst
of the big bang,
nervously humming to itself.
Or to find Christ's cup.
I marveled at its simple gray form,
straining, and at the guilt
of my own weight; but I knew
what would happen if I cut the line.

# Perseus in the Garden

He remembers the snakes in her head,
the cacophony of hisses from her pillow,
each spit venom, some struck
as he reached for her shoulder.
He dreamed of kindness, a summer
storm flashing on the horizon,
he looked away as if to go.
She cursed him, set his mouth
in stone, a statue, a trophy, sorrow-eyed.
He weathered winter ice, became a haven
for earwigs and sow bugs—day upon day
in the waft of a fragrant hell of flowers
opening and shutting their sex.
Spiders knitted him a sweater of captives. Each night she
danced before him, serpentine and writhing among the blooms—
she exaggerated between his stone legs.
Each minute was given to a prayer,
each to a different god, but it was his mind
that became stronger than his belief in stone;
and he moved slowly, grinding, practiced
then more fluently. He left a message
on her venom-soaked pillow—hideous.
She'll swear to anyone who'll listen
that he planted each snake in her head,
fed them mice, and taught them to strike while she innocently
slept. Most afternoons,
she sits in her statuary, talking to an empty
place, talking to the one that got away.

# Afraidness
### *after James Wright*

For thirty years,
since it first crept into me,
I have carried that line;
afraid of its meaning,
never having been quick
with fear.

When I was naked
lying in bed at 3am
its ghost would rise out of me
and paint itself upon the ceiling.

Every day I would contemplate it,
read the poem again and over;
each line a bone in my flesh.

Still I did not understand.

In meditation the line was my mantra,
but I was afraid of being afraid.

This afternoon
after a clap of thunder
and hail beat against this world,
as I sat with my reflection,

I saw it
and my fear
and was not afraid.

I moved my dark hands
around the moon
pulling into my mouth.

With new speed
I smiled brightly

into the sway of darkening grass.

# A Bird History

We lived on the Violent Coast
north of the Sea Lion Kingdoms
in The Great Age of Wind.

Our history was passed down over waves,
on pinions, the unraveling scripts of kelp beds,
an eroding rock bridge along the Great River.

Colored sheets rose from the south
floating as clouds might, but hungry—
that was the season we flew inland.

There had been no word for the forest,
no book of the mountains, but in those
places some of us died.

The new words slowly turning old.

# Why Autumn is the Color of Stone

It begins with Persephone packing her bags,
her inner hive staring out the window.

She sways to the tune of an old sink sky
draining of migratory birds.

Sorrow is chlorophyll in the belly of a goat,
the sour smell of wine, the waft of rot,

and the first scent of wet cement.
The gullies and canals ready for muddy

runs to the sea; their pushiness is like
hunger. She is weary from her mother's green

tirades—had it always been this way?—
a childhood of sheltering and gates,

screening friends and later potential
dates. She mumbles under pendant lights—

What it would be like had she been born a boy,
the god of sticks and thorns? —and writes

no note but checks her bags for all the things
she'll want, then leaves her mother's house,

staring at the hollowed faces of the Medusa
trees in the graying brindle yard.

# The Mud Weavers

The smallest gods of the world
come translucent and falling,
to hit the earth and thus feed it.
They do not answer the farmers,
their weary bone prayers,
nor the bright beaded pleas of dancers.
Both are beggars in the dry dirt.
The smallest gods do not love us— no.
They are the tin roof angels singing
beyond emotions. We are the thirsty soil.

## II. Roots of Ash

# Caliban

Before hatred ate my heart
there was music:
my mother's willow music,
her dark willow music of wind and wave.
There was water singing over
the roots of ash, over stones.

Mother, I am a dead thing
with a voice trained for anything but song,

shackled in magic and pushed down,
taught to speak with a tongue
that damns with belly aches.

Mother, your songs will die within me.
Mother, I am shaped an evil thing.
My tears run for the loss of song.
My fists clench for you.

# West Nile

The birds began to rust,
brown dust, life sparking away.
Starting with one dropped note
like an autumn leaf.
I thought if I buried them,
then a flock might rise up,
come back Lazuren, orphic,
a darker but deeper beauty.
With tunes to conjure the thinking
mind to ice cliffs eroding,
forests blackening,
little harbinger songs—
terrible angelic lurching
dirges that almost fumed
in choking carbon rage.
But nothing comes
so splendidly announced.
The messengers sit Cassandran
in their cells, listening as the first
ship plagues its soldiers onto shore.

# Citizen Kane

we want one word    sometimes    to say something
a mystery    key    magic    the best time of our life
or significance    a word that will    connote our
dreams    or childhood escape    from what we know
we will become    the words    our sacred    secret words
    sweetgrass    hummingbird    seashell    rosebud
        frybread    sweetpea    red ribbon
as we die    and the young    brilliant director    pans
over our lives    using    odd angles    we discover

no one    ever    knew us

# What if Hamlet had Drowned Instead of Ophelia

From beneath the surface with the moon floating on it
I can see the castle lit up with a cheery light
and what appears to be dancing in all the windows.

A wedding? A holiday? What would cause them
to celebrate so without me? I can almost hear
music under the shroud of rain hitting the river.

The houses along my banks are a row of skulls,
their sockets black and they do not reflect—
as I so much liked to do. What am I now?

A martyr? A tragic figure? The reeds sway
until I cannot tell what is green and not my hair.
Have all the villagers gone to the castle party?

Is that Ophelia near the water, being chased by a man—
they both wear masks, perhaps they're mistaken
lovers? Is that what I remember of her laughter or
is that the sound of the small fish nibbling my ear?

# The Magician's Assistant

She hears the grains of the wood box singing
in this darkness that makes her realize she is
the thinnest of air, something that swords
and saw blades only wish they could cut.
She is vaporous, seeping into and out of his mind.

Not a trap door, nor a false panel, not
a mentalist's trick, not a top hat rabbit, she
does not need the whirligig eyes of Mezmer
to do what comes naturally—she is a draft
escaping through the porousness of the world.

And at night, he can hear her all around his house
pushing the leaves, playing the grass and owls,
blowing the shutters and reeding through
the window screens: her symphony of intangibility.
The Magician cannot sleep.  He listens to her;

she is his muse, the oxygen to his flame, just beyond his grasp.

# On Falling and Failing

If Icarus were to speak, he'd kvetch
about long hours of labor over feathers
and wax, listening to Father drone on
about the very nature of quills and paraffin
and where wind and birds originated.
The boy would share his dark fantasy
of proving the old windbag wrong—
jumping up and shouting, Ha!,
 you don't know everything, Dad! —
and the overwhelming sadness
he felt to harbor such thoughts,
which have been bested in depth only
by knowing the old man was,
in fact, right. The underworld
is a naked bed of information, statistics
sheet the sky—doubt is food for the living.
His famous half-minute of descent
is not as vivid to him as the sight
of Father circling for a final fly-by
and shaking his head.

# Iago Says

I swear the scarf he wrapped around his finger
had my name spun in secret threads within.
She was Autumn's orange soul lingering,
hovering over the Ocean like a blossom.
And what did I know of jealousy, except
I've burned from within without logic.
The sun lit our city and I saw its contempt
for all shadows I'd built, all my havoc.
But her hair stroked the wind, balanced the tides
and the stars; within those gilded strands did glide
Pandora's imps to shade my heart and hide
with razor sharp teeth as they shrieked, they cried.
I raged against his house like a hurricane
and unchained the evil his own soul contained.

# The Dark Current

We have lost the shade of blue;
it slipped beneath the night's surface
like a slow immense fish.

I dip my hand into the water
to feel the cool current passing
and you watch me, as if I will reveal

some hidden magic, a bright wonder.
And I think I will remember you like this
with a halo of brightening stars,

smiling, daring me to conjure
a bouquet of delicate birds,
a handful of sparkling seeds.

In this twilight, I could change light
and substance into any gift for you.
But this is enough—

both of us knowing what can be done
for the other, knowing and smiling,
one hand left swimming the dark current.

# Sinking

In the kitchen light she was the sink
waiting for him. He stared at his mute
reflection in stainless steel. She folded
her arms to meet his at the forearms.
His face was a pile of scrap wood left over
from unfinished odd jobs around the house.
She was the brightness of a raw bulb
burning above them. He wanted to squint
but was afraid to send a false signal,
some other meaning than love.

He never saw himself as she did.
She followed him, sometimes he followed her,
to this place. He heard the squeal of every
hinge in the house; she whistled a tune
she'd learned from them. Behind his mouth
was a garbage disposal. She stared at him
with faucet eyes. Sometimes he heard
his father's voice in the chopping noise
as he flipped the switch. He had failed
more than once. But she was never part
of his failure recitals. He felt strange
and lucky around her. There was warmth
where their arms met. They were a water dance
circling the drain before returning to sea.

# Fog Through a Bridge
   *—for Ralph Angel*

Because your body has become fog
rearranging the constellations,
coating the leaves with your breath—
say it's not hard to remember
the incantations that made you this, now.
How many times was smoke written about?—
coursing, billowing up the mirror
toward a reflection you'd never intended.
An isolated girl has written a love sonnet
to your ocean. She's corked the bottle
and thrown it off the bridge.
She counts the seconds
it takes to splash the water,
as if she were mouthing the words
he loves me, he loves me not.

Tonight the skyline is stained
by fire and sirens,
but you focus on the gulls' cries
and the fog horn tearing through you—
a warning, a wicked something
comes this way.
No one sleeps within your arms.
A man sings a drunken love song
which you've heard before,
only backwards or jumbled.
A woman looks at you
like an old friend and you roil.
The immigrants have closed
their shops for the night. Traffic horns
call out like carnival barkers.
You cradle the city like a child
found abandoned on the back step.
No one hears the lullaby you offer
except the alley cats
and one girl counting on a bridge.

# Prospero as TV Weatherman

The broadcast offers no news of the weatherman's plans.
In this winter city populated with fair weather friends,
no one lets him forget the power of his magic is  renowned.
He reaches into the jet stream for another storm to hurtle
against the coast; he casts temperatures and the names
of places onto the images of overtaxed black umbrellas
struggling their way up Market Street; he conjures
a map and with his powerful finger points to a valley;
clouds, as black as his art, begin raining missiles.
Next he summons meteor-sized snowflakes in the east,
blue-faced gods to expel their breaths over the coastline.
And he curses everyone to five more days of the same.

His daughter has grown too bored of stages, cameras,
production assistants, and her make-up wearing father.
Her brow furrows under bright red cumulous hair—
she draws a shining sunflower on the page of her notebook
with all the power needed to move a low pressure system.
He looks upon her and sees his protégé, lineage, dynasty.
But she is a rebellious seed, more artist than antagonist,
and secretly says a prayer: let the tv sets lose their power.

# Present Tension

Facing the Pacific Ocean she says
she loves everything about plate tectonics—
how one continent is shoved by another
wherever they meet, how it is natural
and take millions of years—mountains rise
as others buckle into basins;
but they act as one creature—the living
planet, roaming herds on its back, domination
of galloping brutes butting into each other.
Gone is the happy whole, Pangaea, super
continent, first god, from where the smaller
gods sprouted. I think about her love,
backing away from her violent side
—she expects turmoil like a late date
arriving wet, scuffed, and reeking
of breath mints and beer.

# After the Puma
### for Óscar Wong

The mountain lion breathes a forest,
it roars out aspen and oak
that stretch their branches to the sea—
the leaves are passports,
speaking distance and place.
Each has a tongue of aroma:
musk, wilted blooms, wet rot.
The puma has seen
into the flaming heart of lightning,
has heard the echo and roar of the sea,
knows death is a desert and canyon.
It knows the Earth as a sacred being
who made muscles from mud.
Metal thunders, it screams at the heart
of the hunter—chases her away.
The leaves release a whispered prayer,
Mother of roots give us water
from which we make our tears.

# Why Orpheus Could Not Stay Underground

What was it that drove his ear down—
a chance to change fate?  He felt his way below

to where the rivers carved their own directions
to a shifting coastline of ebony fires.

Around him was the noise of shattering glass, twisting metal.
The specters mouthed their confessions, too late—

forced remorse, bittersweet promises to break.
No one expected music in the darkness,

the dead didn't know what to do—
give him back his love, make the music go away.

All the way back to the surface he throated the black air—
one love song strummed to another

but she did not sing along, nor a sound did she make.
Looking for her he found a wedding gown,

torn, laid upon black rocks like a shadow in reverse.
What good a white dress in a world without light?

It wasn't the silence that made him leave without her,
but a world filled with such horrible noise.

## Lake Light

The best place is near the water's edge
where the swans' white shadows
linger in the tall, offshore reeds.
The chill of dusk pushes long
ripples through the body.

You walk the gravel path an old prospector
smelling gold in everything.
You whistle your father's tune,
happy for the geometry of milkweed,
for the wave rolling slow across the lake.

On muddied knees at the end of the land
you rest. Not a word enters the mind.
Your father once stood here,
watched a fox weave through brush and stone
to steal a drink from its own reflection.
In one breeze you sense what's left of his shadow.

You keep still, accept the shallow breaths
and the cold pain beneath the adam's apple.
You never see a fox. But the white shadows
unfurl from the grassy marsh; their steadiness
shines the last mirrored clouds of daylight.
Your knees sink further into the shore.

# Uncertainty Principle

I do not know the weight of the geese that fly away.
They may be like electrons or other subatomic particles.
I cannot truly know if they are heading south.

More precisely, how can I be sure of my position.
I cannot say how fast the pouting cumulous cloud
to the west is coming, when I will need

to unfold my umbrella. Unable to determine what is
my time, for most of this life I have embraced tardiness,
welcomed the arrival of whim and fancy.

Secretly, I've always fantasized about the atoms
of birds, water, turning leaves: how they all know
where they should be and how long to stay.

# What is Kept in the Heart of the Stone
### *for David Knopfler*

Don't say the word, forgiveness—

it is found written on the tall stones rising
out of the ground like a scolding finger.

Listen: God builds a foundation
of granite and basalt deep in the mud like a rib

humming, vibrating, arcing, reaching up, close
to touch, like desire, aching

for the moment when we can unearth it, hold it
in the hand not as a weapon,

but as one might offer a tongue to a snowflake
or a gift, extended slowly forward

wide-open and without a word.

# III. In Defense of Love

# In Defense of Love

Pictured in the photograph
is an entry wound.

There is no explanation

Love may have struggled

with the victim.         There's no evidence

to support any of this.

I don't think anybody

will suggest Love

is so clever.

Look how
that green shirt was torn.

You almost                reach a point where

you say, Maybe

they're wrong.

Maybe, maybe the night
is so clever,

stalking the day,
not the other way—

the prosecution           totally looked

at the illicit

relationship
and his insurance policy.
Nothing else

has been done but try
to make the evidence fit their theory
of Love   and guilt.

There's nothing wrong

with considering Love
a suspect.
But wrong

to exclude everyone else.

♥ ♥ ♥

In every life there are bullet holes.
Each different from another.
The first shot may have gone

through the victim's chest.
There was a mistake
and we corrected it.

Love's mistake,
we corrected it. We recreated
the situation with simulated tissue.

Remember Dr. Science –
When he was on the stand? –
with all the charts and stuff.

The tissue, Dr. Science says,
we should have used
would have resilience.

Once the bullet penetrates
it ricochets.
It's elastic.          Like the heart.

Whereas we used is a kind of plastic thing
          —a representation of heart—
so once a wound was opened it stayed open.

But we discovered,
it doesn't make any difference.
The elastic stuff that snaps back,

by the time that happens, all the gasses,
all the particles, are lost—
and the bullet is long gone.

So we would like it to be known
that it makes no real difference
between mock hearts, if one snaps back or not.

It's just as good.
Dr. Science did an experiment
and he discovered he didn't like what he found.

♥♥♥

And what did the government of skeleton keywords do?

What words
did they want to find?
Murder,
gun,
blood,
things like that.

So they grew narrow on suspicious sounds.
The prosecutor and police,
they came here to present to you

                                        those words.

The worst words
they could find
to label Love.

There was the word                     red
on February the 14th.
A week later
they call out the word                 murder.

We don't know from what context
these words were abducted,
dragged down to the station house,
kept without water or food
or any sense of time

in an small interrogation room.

Love may have heard them on the radio,
a rap song,
or watched the news that night
or something else
that would have triggered
his fertile mind.

What we do know
is that there aren't any words
to measure the thickness
of the elastic heart
or a self-inflicted wound.

♥ ♥ ♥

What Dr. Psyche said
is nobody is in their right mind
when things can get out
of hand real fast, real easy.

Do you really believe that?
That Love would be like that?
So we don't have context.
We're not sure who called 9-1-1.

♥♥♥

Then there is the business about the songs.
Do you like that kind of music?
I'll be watching you and I'm gonna
make you love me or you will be mine,
you will mine, all mine? You don't know
who sings the next anthem for stalkers.
It may have been Love. It may have been
16 songs in a row.

There was November Rain. There was—
I'm So Excited too. There are songs
that have nothing to do with anything.

And of the 1324 songs Love could have been listening to
on his iPod, it is the lyrics of the 16 downloaded
that afternoon, which were blown up and put on a board
for you and the words like strangle, drown,
shot, kill, murder—they're all highlighted .

How many people don't have something
like that in their music. Let the prosecutor
listen to all your music and see what crimes
he thinks you're capable of.          You know he will
find something sinister.

Because that's what he does.
That's what he's paid to do.
There was no indication that Love thought
the police were coming for his iPod.
Even the prosecution admits
there may have been other songs,
maybe a don't worry, be happy,
or an obla-de-obla-da, or que sera, sera,
because love deleted them on that day.

♥ ♥ ♥

So this is the business of the case:

- selectively cull facts
- ignore their context
- change their meanings
- render everything else meaningless
- draw the sinister inference

When we go back to the crime scene, we:
- look at all the facts
- read the blood evidence
- study the photos and the testimonies,
- understand ballistic reports, the timelines,
- drive the route Love took that night.

♥ ♥ ♥

Now we touch adultery,
even though I don't want to.

I wish it wasn't here,
because it changes everything around.

That's what it does.
The victim was going with another guy.

Living with that guy.
They were making their little things.

Young men, like Love, who are doing well—
good job, lots of money—

start feeling foxy about themselves.
They do things they shouldn't

and he did.

It wasn't anything more than that.
There was never an expression of love.

There was never any thought.
Nothing.

It is what it appears to be.
They saw adultery.   They saw insurance.

Love's guilty,
      they said to themselves walking back

to the police station.
We don't need to see anything else.

It's just a question
of finding the pieces to prove that.

♥ ♥ ♥

There may have been only one shot.
Love couldn't even do that
with one hand.
And you've seen the ballistics.
Consider if that it happened,

here's the scenario you're stuck with:
This wound in the chest

a few inches below a man's nipple;
this thing that looks like
    a defensive wound
like, as Love said, he was grabbing at the gun.
Then, boom, it fires into his palm, comes
out the other side and enters the chest.

What is the significance of that?

If you're going to believe Love shot himself,
then you believe that Love could fake
a self-inflicted injury.
If this is the premeditated crime
that the prosecution suggests would Love
have an affair —and not a secret one—
only a month before his wife's death?
If Love is the person that the government suggests,
would he talk to the police
    when he doesn't have to?
Repeatedly? To this day, Love has never declined
a police interview. Never refused
    to testify.

♥ ♥ ♥

If the crime was premeditated
would Love have downloaded a song like that,

with those kinds of lyrics, the afternoon before?
Would he give the police his computer

without requiring a search warrant?
Would Love not know the precise number

of shots fired if Love had done this crime?
Why would Love say it was just one bang?

Why would Love offer something vague
that the police could seize on

and say, sounds funny.
Why did Love drive 10 miles out of his way?

Why would Love shoot himself
in parts of his body, risk his own death?

Why would Love drag the victim
onto the boardwalk to be so quickly discovered?

Why not under the boardwalk? Or up on the roof?
Why didn't Love steal something?


Or get rid of the gun? Or bury the jewelry?
Love could have thrown her ring in the ocean—

made the whole thing look like a robbery.
Love could have tried to pin it on someone else.


Love called the police
10 miles down the road,

because there are no payphones anymore.
Why would the victim be shot only once?

If it was out of anger, would you not
expect more bullets?  If you wanted

to make sure the victim was dead,
wouldn't you pull the trigger again?

Love wasn't in that car.
Love wasn't crooning the boardwalk.

Love didn't have a gun.  Or a knife.
Love's finger prints were nowhere.

♥ ♥ ♥

There was no evidence
that Love was
ever there.
    You must look
only at the facts
of this investigation.
If there is any doubt at all,
—and who wouldn't
doubt Love—
then we must let Love go.
We must
find:

Love is not guilty of this crime.

## Making Fire

Even after this much evolution,
the furnace dies
and she is cold again.
So I go out to the back of the house,
with its spiders and mosquitoes,
where the rusty gas pipes wait.
I've tightened, lit, re-lit, banged and kicked,
but no rock or bone in my toolkit works.
I snort and swear at the metal box
then look closer at the pilot
and see the stress crack.
Now I know what to do,
but  I can't remove the rusted plate
that keeps me from the pilot.
I go down to the hardware store
where other men with wide hands
pick and prod among the pipes and boards,
grunt and point their calluses at dream tools—
they can't justify the cash.
They linger, tell their fantasy scenarios,
money no limit,
the things they'd build.
I don't belong there;
I buy what I came for and go home.
In fading light I fill the crack
with the metal-repair goo.
It's not pretty, and another guy would scoff,
but I can smell cooking from inside
and I know she appreciates my fire.

# Private Symbology

A V of geese flying through the heart
of Autumn and she responds with bands
of zebra pounding their annual migration
to the north. For each image a herd
of words floods from her page, over
the fingers and up through the arms.

It has taken years of learning to speak
to one another, to comprehend a vast ecology
of the other's mind. What a simple bull finch
might convey to her. How crows could fly
into the underworld of the soul and carry
back messages from the fire-eyed ruler.

O the pelicans in formation over the shore,
a small sandcastle, the feathered rain.
How all this could find him, within
the great desert of his psyche. Where,
wrapped in Bedouin clothes, it takes him days
to travel, through tearing wind and sand.

He writes his cursive lizard tails of love,
such bees hiving their honey of gratitude.
That surf-thrashed sandcastle is enough
for children to build their parapets
of dreams upon. The perch flick their tails,
drawing the pelicans closer, closer.

Each thing they see is a story of devotion,
a reinforcement, something for a passage
to the other. The sea glass is a coin
spent in travel to the City of Sanderlings,
along the spindrift coast of the Pacific,
to deliver the message of a cormorant's plume.

He stops at every church of shells and pebbles
along his path. Above the red tails' soar
under the great cupped hands of the sky.
She will let him drink; she'll soak the fields
and feed him with golden squashes and fruit,
then gesture toward a green carpet to rest upon.

At night, he presses aspen leaves and iris petals
into the pages of a book she wrote to him,
the longest love poem. She borrows the lullaby
of magnolias to sing. He dreams the skin
of kites careening the clouds, ghosting
the letters of words to a cantata, a song of her.

Through the season of leaves grazing the ground
they write their phrases embedded in phrases,
each exciting the other's mind. An inner weather
report delivered entirely in sign language—
curved wrists and fingers, like the inward curl
of the tongue, translating a truer meaning.

# Sky of Sleep

Sometimes she is a tree
to the sky of my sleep,
with long branches to snag
the string or the body of me.

Sometimes I am a kite.
Held there on a hundred windy
days of summer, my edges tear
from the desire to float away.

Birds pick at the string
(useful in the construction of nests),
the crucifixion of bones
against blue sleep,

and somewhere,
in a waking dream,
I make the necessary noises
like snoring to scare them off.

It is enough to be here
in her arms, secure
from drifting,
drifting away.

# Night as a Love Poem

I am your shadow more than
myself, atmosphere without
light, transparent to stars,
this is my comet scar, my Jupiter—
red eye devoted only to your telescope.
I love it best when you reach
with your Hubble, your rockets.
What I give you best is your own
darkness bellied into a bow
pressing onto your landscapes.
Without the curve of you
I would drift into some dark matter.

# The Winter Wolf

There is something a little grayer than the snowed-upon
forest background: a watchfulness, a waiting hunger
in the peripheral vision.  It is not that the white world
is comfortable to her, but she has found a way
to live in it: winter coat, letting the snow form
around her till it is a blanket that keeps her own
warmth within. It is not hard to see she lives
with purpose. This is where my beliefs begin:
she is the mind of snow. She has brought frost
to the pines, ice to the lake, and glitter to
the hills.  Her voice is the wind cutting through
the landscape. When I hear her gospel in the boughs,
I know this is the cathedral, and when her gaze
is upon me, I am already on my knees.

# Coyote Night

The Scotch Broom is spreading rumors of smoke;
and the whispering sparrows say he is a trickster,
but they see him in his chameleon coat,
shifting from dusk to midnight.

Breathless and just as sudden, he stands and scans
the panorama, a ring of green mountains
dusted with the declaration of evening,
listening for the sound of her promise.

It's the hour of the puma padding the ponderosa,
scenting deer through fragrant sap. He could
be a lightning strike, frightening the hare
and the rattlesnake with the belief

of ancient electricity. What can
an owl say in his defense? A beautiful
fool, ruined by love, cries out
each night for reunion, over

the fallen acorns that wait for first rain.

# The Marriage of Tempest and Terra

Each storm in the world a bride
pulling her white dress around her.
She draws her long train down

the ocean aisle. Her eye tightens
as she glides forward. A whirl
of whimsy gathers round her walk.

She is a battle of pressures,
so she strikes out in lightning—
anger passes through her in waves.

Islands rise as though to say,
"It's natural to be nervous," but she
ignores them and speeds her way.

The music of her wedding procession
is that of thunder and torrent,
her ring-bearer swells with pride.

The groom, a dry continent,
has braced himself. He opens
his arms to receive her.

She has quickened her approach,
determined to go to him
and deliver her vows:

*I give my body to join with yours,*
*I will fill your lakes, your riverbeds.*
*And now that we marry,*

*we are the best of ourselves. A place*
*for seeds to sprout. Drink in me—only*
*I can sate you.*

# What Language

I will give her a heron feather
pressed in the folds of a blank book
intended for the longest love poem.
A promise.

In what language do I write
the words that fit her?

I am an uneducated man
feeling out the letters
of a new vocabulary.
I have come to learn
the lexicon of our open field
and speak the petals
of a shared wish,
the circling red tail of desire,
the stones of forgiveness.

I will learn a language
to ask for the wings
of her eyes to fly with me
to the tall grass of our new home.

# Working

> *"...or have I been holding the end of a frayed rope for a thousand years"*
> —James Wright

in the darkness of this conference room
the glow of projected numbers
light up the faces of these analysts

I see other men
who push and pull at ropes
their callused hands burning with each tug

in this stuffy room
oxen are coaxed to pull plows
and with each heavy stone in the earth
we stop
sweat and labor over it
curling our backs to move it
as if the earth had bore us a new burden

and when this stone is gone
we sit in the shade of bamboo
sipping river water
laughing at the new shadows
thrusting up on the horizon
that growing village

in this dim lit room
with its air conditioned hum
the ancient tablets
of lists ledgers and balances
have been recovered
yet not one poem or song
to remember a great flood     the best ox
young lovers

# Coyote and Finch Aubade

This morning an unexpected fog
greets me at the door; the branches
of redwoods and pines seem bodiless
but reaching into my own skin.
I hear the notes of a finch coming
from beyond the blanket of mist.
On the road the coyote stops long
enough to look back at me, as if I
might be slowing him up, keeping him
from his own importance in the world.
I look back, not with coyote reasons,
at your window half-buried beneath
the blanket of waiting stars and new light.
All this hunger and need is a gift
says the song of that nestled finch.

# Island Myths

We were once two islands,
till our species mixed
and created new species.
Your Polynesians
carved their sleek boats
from your trees
to paddle to me and trade
with my aborigines;
like fingers they touched my shore.

They told the myth of you:
alive in the mouth of your volcano;
how you and I are lovers
who ran away together
during the battle of our parents—
yours the gods of land
and mine of sea.
Though we have no fathers,
and may not even be gods,
I think you like that story the best.

# When We Turned the House Into a Ship

So that there were long days of fog and haze
and waves slapping the bow—so much water
like it were a prophecy everywhere you looked.

We gathered up the animals we liked
                          and let them walk the decks

as if they were passengers who booked luxury
travel over the ocean to their new world,
their promised land. And us, the crew,

we spent our time below
                          in the bowels laboring on leaks

and oiling the cogs and levers; and we found ourselves,
in this hard work, closer, more in tune with creaks
and the whines of our walls, so that we knew

things that would go wrong
                          before they happened

and were ready. Each drip became a pool
we bet on—time and size, down to seconds,
down to ounces. When on deck, and at the wheel,

we could judge the birds
                        and tell the distances

to land and ice by flock size and the directions
and altitude they flew. The wind had so many songs
and we learned to whistle each tune like an anthem.

Clouds became maps
                      we studied each wrinkle

looking for something hidden in the topography
a new route that might bring us to riches, to spices.
We loved this being alone with ourselves for long

unending spells on the sea
                     places where our imagination

would build stories from any odd fish, a lone cumulus,
a scrap of someone's hull floating by, or the windless
glassy day itself. We had only to think of why

something had come to be
                     and then everything was

woven into our rich mythology. The Gull King, tired
of wandering the isolated halls of his floating castle,
would sometimes fly in for a visit and we honored him

with bread and nuts from our table.
                     In return, he told us of a strong

good wind we could catch, and so we set to sewing
the small rips in our sails. We sang a prayer
to the sparkling god of the wind, we regifted a feather

tied to our words
                     and felt the air push and rise.

# Honey and Gratitude
   —*after Carlos Martinez Rivas*

Listen to the field of flowers conspire,
like this was your elysian dream,
your small dingy in the stormy sea—
everyone unaware that you are missing.

I have never looked at a rose the same
after you unlocked my eyes to its quiet music,
its whispering lips, its love song of bees
and its butterfly traffic of need.

After reading the honey of your work, I kept
rose petals buried in the shallow grave
of your pages —such a fragrant death—
they died in love and married to your words.

And what do you see now, in your afterlife
of sanguine roses? Those messenger bees
busying phrases back and forth between
the skies of that world and this?

What wave rises from the ocean floor
and swells your flowered boat so close
to the sky, that for the briefest of moments
you might be a cloud, something fluent but vaporous.

Tonight I have pulled my boat onto the shore
of this island of language. Tonight in this place
of traffic, I am a bee in a congregation of bees
gathering your rich golden pollen for my voyage

on the open page of the sea, the lonely hours
between flowers, between storms,
when the bright queen bee of the sun passes
and the hives of stars swarm away.

How do such small bodies do this work—
carrying love across the water, through darkness
to an open ear of petals, an open mouth jeweled
with dew. I shudder with each new bloom of the rose,

the rising and falling, closing and wilting,
undulating in the short strobes of light.
I envy the brief brilliance of the rose,
to be a fast star unique in the universe.

Our bodies are sticky, covered
with the sweet dust, taken so easily
as if we were made for this, only this.
Why whisper it like a secret

when it is the hum and buzzing
that wells up so naturally in our chests?
Why love at all, if we could not feel the grit
of pollen burrowing into our bodies.

Tonight, I am inspired to take my lover's face
into my hands and tell her new words,
deep as water, and give her the deepest kiss,
wing my fingers through her stems of hair,

sail the ocean of her waist,
wander along the blue rivers of her chest,
land softly on the petals of her eyes,
and show my gratitude with this honeyed tongue.

# About the Author

J. P. Dancing Bear is the author of *Conflicted Light* (Salmon Poetry, 2008), *Gacela of Narcissus City* (Main Street Rag, 2006), *Billy Last Crow* (Turning Point, 2004) and *What Language* (Slipstream, 2002), winner of the 2001 Slipstream Prize. His poems have been published in *New Orleans Review, National Poetry Review, Knockout, Bateau, diode, DIAGRAM, Verse Daily* and many others. His work has been ten times nominated for a Puschcart Prize and once for a Forward Prize. He has been working with Nicaraguan poet Blanca Castellon on translating of her poetry into English, the first will appear in *Redactions, Marlboro Review, International Poetry Review, iconoclast* and *The Bitter Oleander*. He has also been working with Mexican poet Oscar Wong to translate his work into English. He is the editor of the *American Poetry Journal* and Dream Horse Press and the host of "Out of Our Minds" a weekly poetry program on public radio station KKUP.